GOODNIGHT TRUMP

GOODNIGHT
TRUMP

An Unauthorized Parody by Totally Failing *New York Times*
Bestselling Authors Erich Origen and Gan Golan. Sad.

LITTLE, BROWN AND COMPANY
New York   Boston   London

In the very classy room

There was a golden mirror

And a silver spoon

And a broadcast of —

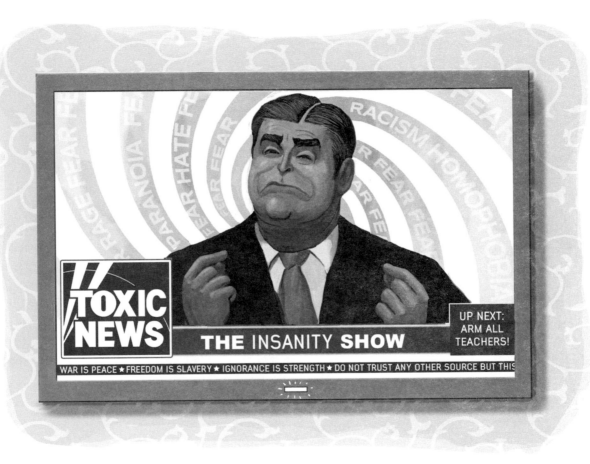

A half-baked story from a fake newsroom

And there were billionaires sending thoughts and prayers

And a pair of manly mittens
And two grabbable kittens

A big beautiful wall
And a Russian nesting doll

A golden seat for tweets in a rush

And a pretty young bunny whom money has hushed

Goodnight classy room

Goodnight heirloom Klan costume

Goodnight cowards kissing up to a buffoon

Goodnight cabinet of whack jobs

Goodnight White House run like the mob

Goodnight drilling in national parks

And goodnight Seven Sins checkmarks

Goodnight undermined law of the land

And goodnight gutted healthcare plan

Goodnight 12 Diet Cokes a day
Goodnight corrosive truth decay

Goodnight very stable genius
Goodnight drawer full of subpoenas

Goodnight bromance with dictators

And goodnight "witch hunt" investigators

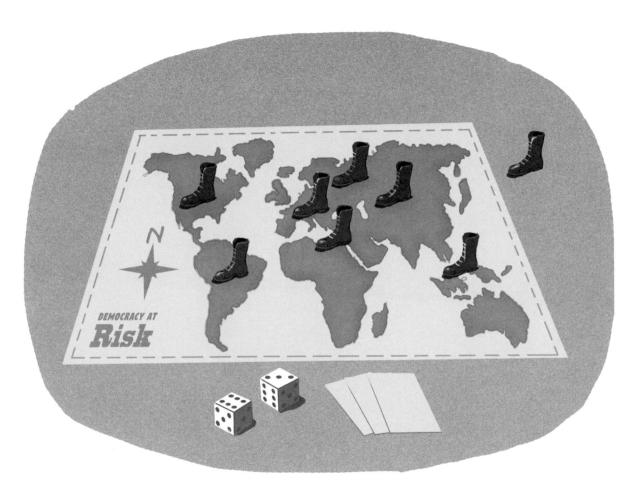

Goodnight democracy at risk

And goodnight blame-game politics

Goodnight army of bots and trolls

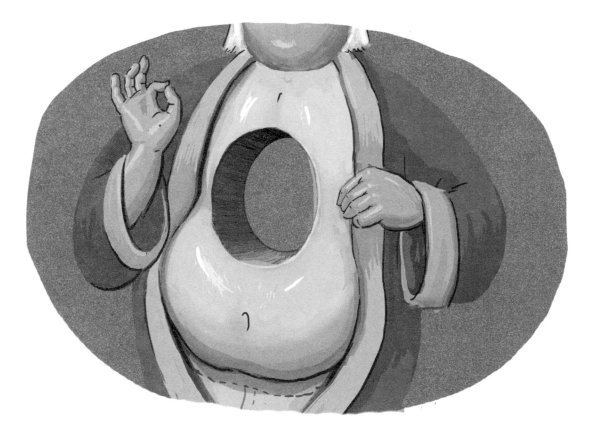

Goodnight hole in the man-child's soul

Goodnight ashamed Lady Liberty
And goodnight shut-out refugees

Goodnight lies that never cease
Goodnight gaslighter-in-chief

Goodnight blacklisted football pros

And goodnight towels thrown at Puerto Rico

Goodnight tariffs and trade wars

Goodnight button much bigger than yours

Goodnight middle-class bait and switch
Goodnight golden showers for the rich

Goodnight Bible stripped of meaning

And goodnight *Art of the Self-Dealing*

Goodnight child held in a cage

And goodnight *I don't care* outrage

Goodnight altered Golden Rule

And goodnight kids gunned down at school

Goodnight global climate shock
Goodnight ticking Doomsday Clock

Goodnight allies thrown under the bus

Goodnight "the best people"

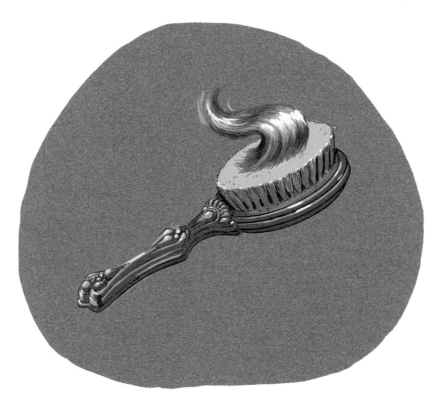

Goodnight cover-up brush

And goodnight to the young bunny
who refused to be hushed

Goodnight swamp

Goodnight troll

Goodnight upended Old Glory
Goodnight hole in the soul

Goodnight to the lies and the truths he evades
Goodnight Trump and his whole sad charade

Afterword

Thank you for reading the greatest book of all time about the greatest and most successful president* of all time. May its tremendous words serve as a soothing incantation.

For generations, the children's book *Goodnight Moon* has helped Americans acquire something scientists call object permanence — the mind-blowing realization that objects you can't see when you close your eyes are still there. Even if you fall asleep, they'll still be there when you wake up. Amazing. We acquire object permanence around the same time we look at a mirror and realize we're seeing a reflection of ourselves. And if you have a golden mirror, it's truly fabulous.

Since the objects we see in *Goodnight Moon* aren't real, but illustrated representations of objects, the book isn't merely helping us acquire object permanence — something else is at play. A ploy by the Deep State or QAnon? Probably. Whatever it is, repetition is key.

Both *Goodnight Moon* and the Trump administration show us that ideas can become real in our minds by virtue of repetition. Whether it's bears in chairs or Obama's Kenyan birth certificate, if you affirm the existence of something enough times, many children (and adults) will believe it.

How many times did the president* tell us that the investigation of him and his associates was a witch hunt? That he was an antiestablishment billionaire? That "nobody knows more" about trade, walls, the Bible, nuclear threats, or taco bowls? Say such things enough times, and people — well, they start to feel very sleepy.

Thankfully, as John Oliver has observed, "The rest of the world continues to exist whether Trump acknowledges it or not."

*

Look for the Helpers

What can you do to repair the world? As Mister Rogers once said, "Look for the helpers." And become one. Search resources like Charity Navigator to find causes you can support with your time, money, or a crowdfunding campaign. Parents, if possible, get your kids involved — service learning fosters leadership and teaches empathy. If you want to model how to participate in our democracy to the fullest, follow the long tradition of heroes who have brought our country closer to its ideals by working to create a flourishing democracy worth protecting.

Organizations that empower children and help protect their rights and well-being include the Alliance for Children's Rights, American Civil Liberties Union (ACLU), Asylum Seekers Advocacy Project (ASAP), Child Foundation, Children's Defense Fund (CDF), Children's Health Fund, Court Appointed Special Advocate Association (CASA), Covenant House, De Anda Legal Fund, Everytown for Gun Safety, Families United 4 Justice, GSA Network, GirlForward, Global Fund for Children, Juvenile Law Center, Kids in Need of Defense (KIND), Little Lobbyists, Malala Fund, National Center for Youth Law (NCYL), National Children's Alliance, National Lawyers Guild (NLG), One Simple Wish, Refugee and Immigrant Center for Education and Legal Services (RAICES), School Justice Project (SJP), Trayvon Martin Foundation, Trevor Project, World Relief, and the Young Center for Immigrant Children's Rights.

And to help build a better world for future generations, get involved with movements for social justice such as By The People, Color of Change, Democratic Socialists of America (DSA), Indivisible, March for Science, People's Action, Movement for Black Lives, Peoples Climate March, Poor People's Campaign, Sunrise Movement, and The Women's March.

This book is dedicated to the children who've been separated from their parents and held in detention centers, refugee children who've been denied asylum, students killed by gun violence, and mothers and infants suffering because they still lack access to healthcare. And to parents who've struggled through so many difficult conversations. We hope *Goodnight Trump* helps you regain your sense of humor and say goodnight.

The following people will be totally #winning a Nobel prize next year

Voldemort, Sauron, Lex Luthor, Ming the Merciless, Emperor Palpatine, General Zod, Doctor Octopus, Bizarro, Bane, Thanos

Our sincere thanks to

Raquel, Lynda, Yuval, Yasmin, Emek, Rosi, Ricardo, The Bean, Lisa, Truman, Jobe, Crissy, Daryl, Sherrod, Robert, George, Mark, Stephani, Andrea, Chris, Mark, Eric, Mary, Rick, Linda, Rose, Bill, Yvonne, Chuck, Jean, Jon, Alex, Sheri, Kim, Aimee, Tina, Betsy, Alexa, Ara, Luann, Christine, Joe, Michael, Neil, Melanie, Debra, John, Heidi, Harry, Miriam, Solomon, Eva, Nicky, Andrew, Mark, Josh H., Josh B., Nato G., Karen, Jeff, Noah, Mike McG, Athena, Favianna, Sam, Tammy, Allen, Pablo, Kei, Rachel, Duncan, Sophie, AFQ, Zina, Ben, Intaba, BMC, Michael S., Reagan A., William, Stormy Daniels, Colin Kaepernick, Pantone color, Carrie Fisher, George Michael, Anthony Bourdain, David Bowie, Fred Rogers, and of course Margaret and Clement

Other books by Origen & Golan

The Adventures of Unemployed Man
Les aventures d'Ultra-chômeur
Don't Let the Republican Drive the Bus!
Goodnight Bush

Little, Brown and Company
Hachette Book Group
1290 Avenue of the Americas, New York, NY 10104
littlebrown.com

First Edition: November 2018

Little, Brown and Company is a division of Hachette Book Group, Inc. The Little, Brown name and logo are trademarks of Hachette Book Group, Inc.

The publisher is not responsible for websites (or their content) that are not owned by the publisher.

The Hachette Speakers Bureau provides a wide range of authors for speaking events. To find out more, go to hachettespeakersbureau.com or call (866) 376-6591.

ISBN 978-0-316-53113-9
LCCN 2018956697

10 9 8 7 6 5 4 3 2 1

PHX

Printed in the United States of America